The Dream Journal

THE DREAM PACK

The Dream Journal

A Record of Your Dreams

 Reader's Digest

THE READER'S DIGEST ASSOCIATION, INC.
NEW YORK LONDON MONTREAL SYDNEY CAPE TOWN

A READER'S DIGEST BOOK

Created and produced by Duncan Baird Publishers, London

Copyright © 1997 Duncan Baird Publishers
Text copyright © 1997 Duncan Baird Publishers
Commissioned artwork copyright © 1997 Duncan Baird Publishers

ISBN 0-89577-972-2

Editorial consultant Peggy Vance
Editor Judy Dean
Designers Jeniffer Harte, Lucie Penn
Commissioned artwork Alison Jay, Nick Dewar, Jeniffer Harte
Jacket design Jeniffer Harte

The Dream Journal is part of The Dream Pack and must not be
sold separately.

Reader's Digest and the Pegasus logo are registered trademarks of
The Reader's Digest Association, Inc.

Printed in China by Imago

Keeping a Record

How many of all the dreams you have ever had in your life can you recall clearly? Can you even remember the dream you had last night? Perhaps you have a half-memory of a handful of dreams from the past – even from your childhood – and of one or two more recent ones. Sometimes just a single scene will linger through your waking hours for a day or two before it fades from your mind like most of the others. Or perhaps you remember only nightmares or anxiety dreams, in which the emotions that you experienced were stark, strong, and threatening.

The best way to hold on to your dream life in all its fullness and variety is to keep this Dream Journal. We are all familiar with the elusive character of our dreams: in the very moment of waking, we begin to sense them receding, and ten minutes later we can usually remember only about 30 percent of their content. But if you write down your dreams just after waking, you may be able to capture and preserve these precious messages from the unconscious. Spend the first few minutes of wakefulness prospecting for the precious dust before it drifts away on the breeze of mundane affairs. You will never regret the small effort this takes. Your reward, to continue the gold-rush metaphor, will be a valuable claim staked on the vast lode of the inner self. Having built up your dream record morning by morning, you will gain for yourself a fascinating archive of the unconscious. With telling and extensive evidence at your disposal, you will be well equipped to trace connections, identify submerged preoccupations, decipher archetypes and symbols, and explore your deepest desires, your strongest instincts and your most complex inner tensions – as well as charting how all these things change with the passage of time.

Conceived as a unique log of your journey toward enhanced self-knowledge, the Dream Journal will prove also to be a vital aid on the road to realizing your full psychological potential.

If you think of the journal as the novel of your dreaming self, then the individual dreams are its chapters, separate and yet connected, each revealing another aspect of the story.

The practice of recording and interpreting dreams is beneficial not only for the record you create, but also because it exercizes the imagination. With time, your powers of dream recall will become stronger and your skill at interpretation will improve. At first you will probably record only fragments of dreams – blurry, broken episodes, accompanied by vague feelings that you cannot precisely describe. But more and more, you will be able to remember full and complex dreams in all their subtlety – not only visually, but sometimes through the recollection of other senses too.

Similarly, your first interpretations may involve a large element of guesswork, but you will feel increasingly secure in your readings as you accumulate more data and receive confirmation of some of your initial suppositions (although others, of course, will turn out to be mistaken). In time you may find that you develop a "feeling" for the significance of certain dreams – or in other words, your understanding will grow instinctively.

The principal requirement in keeping the Dream Journal is honesty – the ability to resist making adjustments to memory for the sake of making your dreams more interesting, palatable, or coherent. Avoid, also, the temptation to impose significance too soon: ideally, your entries should be dotted with question marks, denoting tentative answers to be filled in later – perhaps only after your journal is full. Premature conclusions can throw you off the trail for ever. On the other hand, you must have the courage to make plausible guesses. Every guess is a brave step forward into the shadowy realm of the self. Luck in your quest will not be needed: the degree of success that you enjoy will be a direct reflection of your perseverance, open-mindedness and eagerness to know the truth.

How to Use
the Dream Journal

The first rule of keeping a dream journal is not to attempt to be over-tidy – try to relish the random clustering of notes. On the left page, the headings will help you to organize background information. The right page is blank, for you to write down your dream, with drawings if you wish. Your interpretation is best recorded on this page too, keyed into the details of the dream account.

Alternative approaches

The journal can be filled in chronologically, yielding a numbered sequence of dreams so that you can trace the development of your dream life over time. The color illustrations (left pages) will seldom be directly relevant to your dream, but by exploring the relationship between the two, even if this is one of contrast, you may well hit upon some illuminating insights.

Alternatively, choose the illustration that most resembles your dream experience, and make your record on the pages where that illustration occurs.

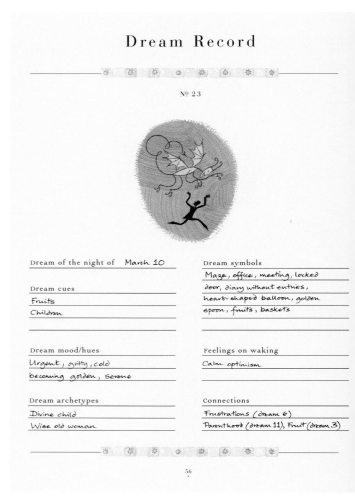

Dream Record

№ 23

Dream of the night of	March 10

Dream cues
Fruits
Children

Dream mood/hues
Urgent, gritty, cold
becoming golden, serene

Dream archetypes
Divine child
Wise old woman

Dream symbols
Maze, office, meeting, locked
door, diary without entries,
heart-shaped balloon, golden
spoon, fruits, baskets

Feelings on waking
Calm optimism

Connections
Frustrations (dream 6)
Parenthood (dream 11), Fruit (dream 3)

56

Then, use the notes page at the back of the journal to make a chronological listing of your dreams: write down the date along with the dream number. Don't worry that your choice of

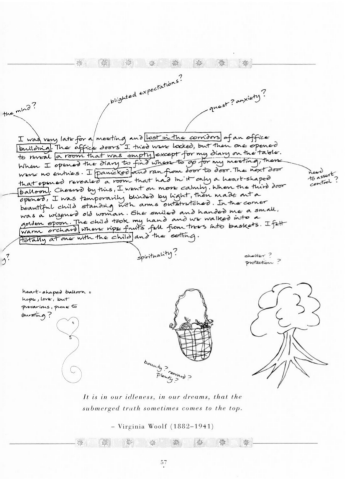

the mind?

blighted expectations?

quest? anxiety?

I was very late for a meeting and lost in the corridors of an office building. The office doors I tried were locked, but then one opened to reveal a room that was empty except for my diary on the table. When I opened the diary to find where to go for my meeting, there were no entries. I panicked and ran from door to door. The next door that opened revealed a room that had in it only a heart-shaped balloon. Cheered by this, I went on more calmly. When the third door opened, I was temporarily blinded by light, then made out a beautiful child standing with arms outstretched. In the corner was a wizened old woman. She smiled and handed me a small, golden spoon. The child took my hand and we walked into a warm orchard where ripe fruits fell from trees into baskets. I felt totally at one with the child and the setting.

need to assert control?

spirituality?

shelter? protection?

heart-shaped balloon = hope, love, but precarious, prone to bursting?

bounty? reward? plenty?

It is in our idleness, in our dreams, that the submerged truth sometimes comes to the top.

– Virginia Woolf (1882–1941)

57

illustration will become more limited as the journal fills up: perhaps the last picture – the one you are *forced* to use – has some special significance related to your innermost preoccupations?

Dream cues
Record the key features of your dream. To prompt these themes another night, hold them in your mind before sleep.

Dream mood/hues
Write down adjectives or associations (including colors) that seem to you to capture the overall mood of each dream.

Dream archetypes
List any possible archetypes from your dream (see Archetype Cards).

Dream symbols
Identify any themes, objects or actions that may be symbolic (see Dream Book, pages 50–53, and Dream Action Cards).

Feelings on waking
These feelings may relate to the dream's last scene, rather than its overall mood.

Connections
Note any related dreams that you have recorded elsewhere in the journal.

The
Dream Journal

The Dream Record (pages 12–79) invites you to log and
interpret your dreams. Gradually building up to become a vista,
in words and pictures, of your innermost self, this is the key
to your unconscious – which you may explore time and again to
reach a fuller understanding of your own hidden motivations.
In the Personal Dream Directory (pages 80–87), you may create
your own dictionary of the most prevalent symbols of your
dreams. Finally, Dream Talk (pages 88–95) is a space for you
to record the valuable insights of dream interpretation performed
with the help of a friend or partner.

Dream Record

Dream of the night of

Dream cues

Dream mood/hues

Dream archetypes

Dream symbols

Feelings on waking

Connections

To work with ... dreams, one must cultivate humility and the ability to tinker.

– Stephen A. Martin (1992)

Dream Record

Nº 2

Dream of the night of

Dream symbols

Dream cues

Dream mood/hues

Feelings on waking

Dream archetypes

Connections

Dream Record

Dream of the night of

Dream cues

Dream mood/hues

Dream archetypes

Dream symbols

Feelings on waking

Connections

A dream that is not understood
is like a letter not opened.

The Talmud

Dream Record

Dream of the night of
....

Dream cues
....
....
....

Dream mood/hues
....
....

Dream archetypes
....
....

Dream symbols
....
....
....
....

Feelings on waking
....
....

Connections
....
....

Dream Record

Dream of the night of
....

Dream cues
....
....
....
....

Dream mood/hues
....
....
....

Dream archetypes
....
....
....

Dream symbols
....
....
....
....
....

Feelings on waking
....
....
....

Connections
....
....
....

If you bring forth what is within you,
What you bring forth will save you.
If you do not bring forth what is within you,
What you do not bring forth will destroy you.

Gospel of Thomas, Apocrypha

Dream Record

Dream of the night of

Dream symbols

Dream cues

Dream mood/hues

Feelings on waking

Dream archetypes

Connections

Dream Record

N⁰ 7

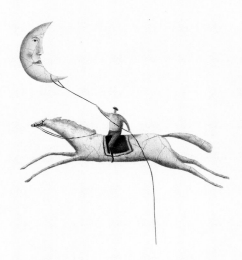

Dream of the night of
_____

Dream cues
_____
_____
_____
_____

Dream mood/hues
_____
_____
_____

Dream archetypes
_____
_____
_____

Dream symbols
_____
_____
_____
_____
_____

Feelings on waking
_____
_____
_____

Connections
_____
_____
_____

In dreams we catch glimpses of a life larger than our own.

– Helen Keller (1947)

Dream Record

№ 8

Dream of the night of

Dream cues

Dream mood/hues

Dream archetypes

Dream symbols

Feelings on waking

Connections

Dream Record

Nº 9

Dream of the night of

Dream symbols

Dream cues

Dream mood/hues

Feelings on waking

Dream archetypes

Connections

Once upon a time, I, Chuang-tzu, dreamed I was a butterfly,
fluttering hither and thither ... Suddenly I was awakened ...
Now I do not know whether I am a man who dreamed he was a
butterfly, or whether I am a butterfly now dreaming I am a man.

– Chinese sage (*c.*100BC)

Dream Record

Nº 10

Dream of the night of

Dream cues

Dream mood/hues

Dream archetypes

Dream symbols

Feelings on waking

Connections

Dream Record

Nº 11

Dream of the night of

Dream cues

Dream mood/hues

Dream archetypes

Dream symbols

Feelings on waking

Connections

For it is dreams that lift us to the flowing,
changing world that the heart longs for.

– W.B. Yeats (1865–1939)

Dream Record

Dream of the night of

Dream symbols

Dream cues

Dream mood/hues

Feelings on waking

Dream archetypes

Connections

Dream Record

Nº 13

Dream of the night of

Dream cues

Dream mood/hues

Dream archetypes

Dream symbols

Feelings on waking

Connections

If a man sees himself in a dream plunging in a river: good,
it means purification from all evil.

Ancient Egyptian dream book

Dream Record

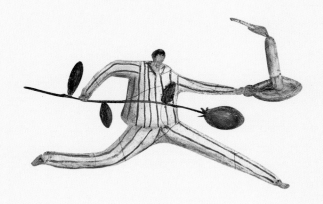

Dream of the night of

Dream symbols

Dream cues

Dream mood/hues

Feelings on waking

Dream archetypes

Connections

Dream Record

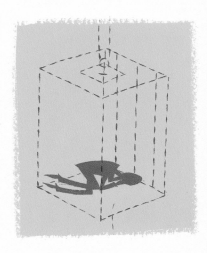

Dream of the night of

Dream symbols

Dream cues

Dream mood/hues

Feelings on waking

Dream archetypes

Connections

Dreams are the facts from which
we must proceed.

– C.G. Jung (1875–1961)

Dream Record

Dream of the night of

Dream cues

Dream mood/hues

Dream archetypes

Dream symbols

Feelings on waking

Connections

Dream Record

Dream of the night of

Dream cues

Dream mood/hues

Dream archetypes

Dream symbols

Feelings on waking

Connections

Something we were withholding made us weak
until we found it was ourselves.

– Robert Frost (1874–1963)

Dream Record

No 18

Dream of the night of

Dream cues

Dream mood/hues

Dream archetypes

Dream symbols

Feelings on waking

Connections

Dream Record

Nº 19

Dream of the night of

Dream symbols

Dream cues

Dream mood/hues

Feelings on waking

Dream archetypes

Connections

Our truest life is when we are in dreams awake.

– Henry Thoreau (1817–1862)

Dream Record

Dream of the night of

Dream symbols

Dream cues

Dream mood/hues

Feelings on waking

Dream archetypes

Connections

Dream Record

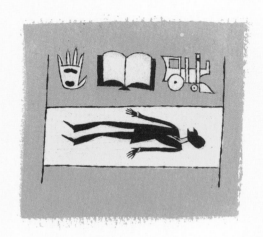

Dream of the night of

Dream symbols

Dream cues

Dream mood/hues

Feelings on waking

Dream archetypes

Connections

Sender of true oracles,
While I sleep send me your unerring skill
To read what is and what will be.

From a Greek magical papyrus

Dream Record

Dream of the night of

Dream symbols

Dream cues

Dream mood/hues

Feelings on waking

Dream archetypes

Connections

Dream Record

Dream of the night of

Dream symbols

Dream cues

Dream mood/hues

Feelings on waking

Dream archetypes

Connections

It is in our idleness, in our dreams, that the submerged truth sometimes comes to the top.

– Virginia Woolf (1882–1941)

Dream Record

No 24

Dream of the night of

Dream symbols

Dream cues

Dream mood/hues

Feelings on waking

Dream archetypes

Connections

Dream Record

Dream of the night of

Dream cues

Dream mood/hues

Dream archetypes

Dream symbols

Feelings on waking

Connections

A dream that is not understood remains a mere occurrence;
understood, it becomes a living experience.

– C.G. Jung (1875–1961)

Dream Record

Dream of the night of

Dream cues

Dream mood/hues

Dream archetypes

Dream symbols

Feelings on waking

Connections

Dream Record

Dream of the night of

Dream symbols

Dream cues

Dream mood/hues

Feelings on waking

Dream archetypes

Connections

*The spirit of man has two dwelling places: both
this world and the other world. The borderland
between them is the third, the land of dreams.*

Brihad Aranyaka Upanishad

Dream Record

Dream of the night of

Dream cues

Dream mood/hues

Dream archetypes

Dream symbols

Feelings on waking

Connections

Dream Record

Dream of the night of

Dream symbols

Dream cues

Dream mood/hues

Feelings on waking

Dream archetypes

Connections

Dreams are a drama taking place on one's own interior stage.

– C.G. Jung (1875–1961)

Dream Record

Dream of the night of

Dream symbols

Dream cues

Dream mood/hues

Feelings on waking

Dream archetypes

Connections

Dream Record

Dream of the night of

Dream symbols

Dream cues

Dream mood/hues

Feelings on waking

Dream archetypes

Connections

Those who lose dreaming are lost.

Australian Aboriginal saying

Dream Record

Dream of the night of

Dream symbols

Dream cues

Dream mood/hues

Feelings on waking

Dream archetypes

Connections

Dream Record

N? 33

Dream of the night of

Dream cues

Dream mood/hues

Dream archetypes

Dream symbols

Feelings on waking

Connections

*The dream ... is a texture woven of time and
space inside which we find ourselves.*

– Robert Bosnack (1988)

Dream Record

Dream of the night of

Dream symbols

Dream cues

Dream mood/hues

Feelings on waking

Dream archetypes

Connections

Personal
Dream Directory

*Published dream directories serve as guides to the interpretation of some
of the symbols that you will have noted in your Dream Record, but the
significance of each symbol can only be fully understood in light of your
own life circumstances, both generally and at the time of the dream.
Here you have an opportunity to create your own symbols directory, in
each case listing the symbol's meaning and the dream or dreams in
which it occurs (cross-refer to these under Connections).*

Symbol _____

Notes _____

_____

_____

_____

Connections _____

_____

Symbol _____

Notes _____

_____

_____

_____

Connections _____

_____

Symbol

Notes

Connections

Symbol

Notes

Connections

Symbol

Notes

Connections

Symbol

Notes

Connections

Symbol

Notes

Connections

Symbol

Notes

Connections

Symbol

Notes

Connections

Symbol

Notes

Connections

Symbol

Notes

Connections

Symbol

Notes

Connections

Symbol

Notes

Connections

Symbol

Notes

Connections

The Dream Journal

Symbol

Notes

Connections

Symbol

Notes

Connections

Symbol

Notes

Connections

Symbol

Notes

Connections

Personal Dream Directory

Symbol ....

Notes ....

....

....

....

Connections ....

....

Symbol ....

Notes ....

....

....

....

Connections ....

....

Symbol ....

Notes ....

....

....

....

Connections ....

....

Symbol ....

Notes ....

....

....

....

Connections ....

....

Symbol

Notes

Connections

Symbol

Notes

Connections

Symbol

Notes

Connections

Symbol

Notes

Connections

Personal Dream Directory

Symbol

Notes

Connections

Symbol

Notes

Connections

Symbol

Notes

Connections

Symbol

Notes

Connections

Dream Talk

The following eight pages have been set aside for you to record the
conclusions drawn from some of your dream talk. Write down the
number of your dream (shown at the top of each Dream Record page)
and the confidant(e) with whom you have discussed it. In the empty
space below, describe in words and/or evoke in drawings the
interpretations and enlightenments revealed in your conversation.

Dream number   Dream talk with

Insights

Dream Talk

Dream number

Dream talk with

Insights

Dream number

Dream talk with

Insights

89

The Dream Journal

Dream number

Dream talk with

Insights

Dream number

Dream talk with

Insights

Dream Talk

Dream number

Dream talk with

Insights

Dream number

Dream talk with

Insights

Dream number

Dream talk with

Insights

Dream number

Dream talk with

Insights

Dream Talk

Dream number

Dream talk with

Insights

Dream number

Dream talk with

Insights

The Dream Journal

Dream number

Dream talk with

Insights

Dream number

Dream talk with

Insights

Dream Talk

Dream number

Dream talk with

Insights

Dream number

Dream talk with

Insights

Notes